RED EARTH
and
Other Poems

Adamu Ajunam

Published by
AMV Publishing Services
P.O. Box 661 Princeton NJ 08542
Tel(s): 6095770905 & 7326476721 Fax: 6097164770
www.amvpublishingservices.com
customerservice@amvpublishingservices.com

in association with

Anthill Global Nigeria Ltd.
55 Femi Ayantuga Crescent
Suru-Lere Lagos Nigeria
Tel: +234 08060314519
www.anthillglobal.com
adamuajunam@anthillglobal.com

Red Earth and Other Poems
Copyright © 2012 Adamu Ajunam

All rights reserved. No part of this publication may be reproduced, stored in a retrieval system, or transmitted in any form or by any means, electronic, mechanical, photocopying, recording or otherwise without the written permission of the copyright holder.

Cover Photo & Concept: Adamu Ajunam
Book & Cover Design: AMVPS

Library of Congress Control Number: 2011961325

ISBN: 0-9766941-7-4 (10-Digit)
        978-0-9766941-7-5 (13-Digit)

CONTENTS

Introduction 6
Foreword 9
Red Earth 13
Going Back in Time 15
The Return to Goree 17
Queen Amina 19
Words 20
Justice 21
Wura 22
Love or Leave Her 23
The Yoruba Dancer 24
Where is The Love? 25
The Decline 26
To the Bird 27
Moments 28
Moonlight Night 29
Nwanne 30
Bargains 31
Enjoy a Coke 34
The Regret of Mungo Park 35
This Generation 37
The Next Generation 39
Lagos under Siege 40
Our Different Leaders 41
The Third World 42
Beautiful Nubia 43
Untimely Death 44
My Sin with Time 46
Shaka The Zulu 47
Lagos Life 48

Poverty 49
Vip Road Closure 50
The Nigerian Factor 51
The Lost Smile 52
After the Boom 53
To Be Born Today 54
The Mobile Tailor 55
Social Security 57
The Day of Creation 58
Love Theme 59
Requiem 60
The Garden 61
Salute To Queen Nzinga 62
Jogging Rhyme 63
Peace 64
City Explosion 65
May 66
Decadence 67
Go Slow 68
Power Tussle 70
Abuja 71
Stalemate 73
Our Burden 74
The Voice in the Wind 75
Quick Money 76
Tribute To Philip Emeagwali 77
Dividends of Democracy 78
The African Time 79
Molue Palaver 80
All is Well 81
Shadows in The Night 82
The Secret of Eulogy 83
Follow Me 84
Lost Opportunity 86
Ritual Murderers 87

Armchair Critics 88
The People's Prayer 89
Harmattan Blues 90
Zealots in the Mainstream 91
Askia Mohammed 93
The Gates Of Kano City 95
The Atilogwu Dancer 96
My Pearl 97
Phantom Coup 99
The Idler 100
Good Morning 102
Area Boy 103
The Locust Years 104

INTRODUCTION

This book is a collection of poems which I started writing about ten years ago. It has taken this long because of the tight schedule I have between my profession as Engineer and my other passions. Even though it was not calculated to be so, the delay gave me the opportunity to be critical about my work resulting in amendments, recasting or outright rejection of some of the poems. I have decided to release the poems now following the positive comments and encouragement I received from close friends to whom I had showed the draft. They admonished me and wondered why I had locked up my thoughts in a closet when I should be sharing them with the rest of the world. I am encouraged even more by the humble success recorded by my recent publications; "Eko – The Navel of The Giant" and "Nigeria: A Harvest of Nature" - which are both tourist guides.

This collection can be subdivided into three themes namely, Africa, Nigeria and tributes to some of the continent's great legends. The Nigerian category dwells on leadership, citizenry and their relationship as we journey in the process of evolving into a nation. The title poem, "Red Earth", is dedicated to my country, Nigeria and it reflects on the different entities within our dear nation.

Poetry is very emotional and spiritual. This is why I choose to write in free verse, to allow me the flexibility to express, in an intimate way, the many experiences that have aroused my interest. As a professional engineer and photographer, I find poetry very engaging, colourful and a creative enterprise that has offered me the opportunity to look critically at issues from another perspective.

Living in Nigeria in spite of the very harsh conditions can somewhat be rewarding in terms of personal growth. It opens the window for the mind to become innovative and creative in finding new approaches to solve life's problems. It is the probe into how Nigerians go about their daily lives trying to get answers that have consumed my desires and thoughts in many of the poems. Some of the poems like "Love or Leave Her" show the interplay of love and the frustration the people encounter. Another poem, "The Nigerian Factor", demonstrates the negative energy expended each day trying to frustrate many genuine efforts that can bring glory to the country.

We have a very rich culture which, unfortunately, we celebrate half-heartedly or ignore outright. We are yet to tap into our diverse and rich cultural repertoire, which include music and dance. The poems "Yoruba Dancer" and "Atilogwu Dancer" are tributes to Nigerian culture.

Nigeria and indeed Africa have had their fair share of great leaders, not the sit-tight types that have become common place today, so-called leaders who have nothing to move our continent forward. We have had great men and women at the helm of affairs who have proven their abilities as good leaders in the past. Their stories should motivate today's men and women to aspire to greatness. A few poems like "Shaka the Zulu", "Queen Amina" and "Salute to Queen Nzinga" are tributes to worthy icons.

The major influences on my style have been the attention to discipline impacted on me by my father, and the writings of Jacque Prevert, the French poet and Pablo Neruda, the Chilean poet. I am greatly inspired by Prevert's poems, which begin with simple narration only to make unexpected turns to a unique observation.

There has been also some experimentation in the style, particularly in "Bargain", which is written mainly in ten-line stanzas. All the poems in this category attempt to demonstrate the proactive and the participatory nature of Nigerian culture.

Finally, I cannot conclude this introduction without paying tribute to all those who support me daily in one way or the other to succeed in my endeavours. The first person who would have received the first finished copy would have been my late father, Mr. Nicholas Ajunam. He gave all the lessons that guide me today on appreciation of orderliness. He taught me how to appreciate, departmentalize and use time. I remain ever grateful that I had a teacher in him. I always remain thankful to my brothers and sisters for their love and kindness.

I am thankful to my friends and colleagues, particularly Engr. Nat Ikem for his excellent team spirit. You are such a wonderful listener and a heart full of humility. I will not forget my proof reader, Mrs. Boladele Dapo-Thomas of Five Talents Proofreaders, whose unique approach to criticism guides me to write what others can understand. Many thanks also go to Dr. Ruben Abati of the Guardian Newspaper and Professor Aderemi Raji-Oyelade of the University of Ibadan for their contributions to this work.

And last but not the least is my family, whose presence not only excites me but also motivates me to work. I hope these few lines will bring smiles to your faces now that it is down. Thank you Valerie and Barak my adorable angels.

Adamu Ajunam
Lagos,
January 2011

Adamu Ajunam

FOREWORD

It is with great pleasure and honour that I respond to the author's request to write a few words on his book "Red Earth".

When I met Adamu in 1983, I saw a young promising engineer, well-trained and educated with First and Master's Degrees in Engineering from reputable institutions in Europe and United States respectively. His search for knowledge also took him to Germany where he lived for a while and learnt German which he speaks and writes fluently. It was therefore only natural that he was employed as a senior staff of Julius Berger Nigeria PLC, the construction company with high regard for its quality of staff. In no time, I recognized that Engineer Ajunam had more to offer than engineering.

Clearly a man of many parts, Adamu Ajunam the photographer was soon revealed. I learnt of his passion for photography, which he said dated back to his childhood when he would focus on objects with an imaginary camera. He possesses a Diploma in Photography from the New York Institute of Photography. Engineer Ajunam proved his mettle and photographic skills with his works adorning Julius Berger's Annual Reports and Calendars. Among the pictures were some really impressive images - I remember vividly one with the fisherman flinging his net into the Lagos Lagoon with the Eko Bridge in the background. In my many conversations with Engineer Ajunam, I learnt that he had another artistic passion: painting. He explained to me that engineering, photography and painting were all arts referring to the same subjects of humanity, history and culture, but every profession in its own manner.

Engineer Ajunam has in many ways proven his engineering skills and demonstrated his leadership qualities over the years.

With "Red Earth" Engineer Ajunam has systematically put together the many facets of the man Adamu Ajunam- as an Engineer and Artist - with a collection of poems which brings out clearly to all who love Nigeria and its essence –the culture, its beauty, ideals, vision, inspiration, driving force and rich heritage.

He has once again, after the success of his two earlier publications- "EKO the Navel of The Giant" (2004) and "Nigeria, a Harvest of Nature" published in 2010, shown the world "his beloved Nigeria" as he- the diehard optimist – sees it.

Thank you very much "A.A" and may God continue to bless you.

Engineer Ludwig Haussmann
Former Managing Director
Julius Berger Nigeria PLC

Poems

RED EARTH

Red earth, dear earth
I could not have been made
From any other earth
For this is the only earth
When I stand on
That makes me feel whole.
When I walk on another
In distant lands,
Some strangeness overwhelms me
My feet stumble
My heart turns heavy
I lose the warmth and feel insecure
But when I am surrounded by red earth
My feet are firm
My spirit is buoyed
And I can soar in the sky
I do not fear to sleep
In the royal red in Ikpoba Hill
And revitalize my blood
The powers that cast the Zuma Rock
Have hardened the marrows of my bones
The mirror that shines in Oguta Lake
Will reflect my face with no difference
Like the sparkling waters of Bagauda Lake
I do not fear the zealots
I meet within
But scamper for life from hypocrites
Worrying about the colour of my skin
There is finality of purpose that beckons
When I breathe the air

Oozing from the pores of red earth
Where I am free from any discrimination
I was born on red earth
I grew on red earth
And I cherish to know
That a grain such as I
Finds a place in this land
And when I am no more
I know unto this red earth
Shall I return, carried like dust
Not beyond the frontiers of my native land.

Adamu Ajunam

GOING BACK IN TIME

I went out searching for USA
Four thousand years ago
No map I found could help
The mighty land today
That has a pie in almost every land on earth
Christopher Columbus sighted the land
Great minds unified the land
If we stretch the mind, it seems not long ago
Four thousand years so distant
I found a great land on the Nile
The cradle of civilization
They drove themselves to nuts
In search of the human limits
They wondered why man would not live forever
Not finding any answers
They mummified the body
This remains mum till date, as only testimony
Wisdom spread like wild fire on every inch of land
The gale has calmed and the seeds are buried
In the desert dunes
The land of the Pharaohs was once so fertile
And great thoughts sprang like mushroom everywhere
But now dark clouds do gather over her sky
And her people are seen as only common.
Although they removed the cruel curtain
Man knew then as dark ages.
They unchained the power for thoughts
And journeyed deep into the mystery of man
They were never in doubt life is a continuum
The hunger for knowledge they could not ease

Learning from a plane was only half backed
To get the bird's eye view
Thoughts gave birth to the pyramid
To reach an overview,
Where all remain awe-inspiring
Four thousand years of harshness
The pyramids still remain a pride
The shadow that runs behind the sun
They found as clue of priceless watches
The Nile rustles and continues to flow
We wait to hear the echo
When will man return to his roots, simple equality of man.

Adamu Ajunam

THE RETURN TO GOREE*

I have wondered sufficiently
Why return to this port
This port that resurrects in me
Hate that I have relinquished
Fear that I have overcome
And tears my eyes can no more find

I have wondered sufficiently
What thoughts my mind would engage
In the place my brother lost his roots
His freedom was axed like an unwanted wood
His eyes were plucked to dream more
And sold for a despicable fee

I have wondered sufficiently
How much residue from that fatality still follows me
The struggle I need to rehabilitate my broken ego
Why the pains of the denials do not drive me mad
My ambition to excel must not be for a moment
And there is no god that takes my cup

I have wondered sufficiently
Why I have not long returned to Goree to pick the pieces
To learn to see life like china ware
To worry about tomorrow, this is divine
To stand to fight and displace the emptiness
That voids my hopes to bear great dreams

I have wondered sufficiently
And will return to Goree to see the future
To remind my enemies of a promise never wished away
Only gold that has been through fire can be pure
That in every day is a new beginning
And yesterday like the dead will take care of itself.

*Goree is an Island off the coast of Senegal. It was a major slave depot for over three hundred years from 1536 to the time when the French halted it. The French called it Goree meaning "good harbour", even though the crimes committed against humanity, particularly the blackman here continue to affect his freedom.

Adamu Ajunam

QUEEN AMINA*

When Amina comes again
She won't look at the indifferent and venal women
Nor listen to the indolent and hypocrite
She will care less for those who only follow the wind.

When Amina comes again
She will cage and strip the men
Who have married us to shame and degradation
She will banish them all who live without a conscience.

When Amina comes again
She will disrobe the trusted fathers
Whose support has helped corrupt the system
And let us float like a rudderless boat.

When Amina comes again
She will seize and eliminate the women
Who breed the cantankerous children
Who fearlessly encourage anarchy.

When Amina comes again
She will ride a chariot of fire to renew her battle
She will wipe off all nefarious persons
Who block the shinning path of justice.

When Amina comes again
She will gather all the children and let them know
That if fear consumes their hearts
Life will be desolate without a home and freedom.

*Queen Amina of Zazzau was a great warrior who ruled the original seven states of Hausaland in the 16th century.

WORDS

With the cry of a new born child
We welcome with joy the advent of a voice
A voice that may wrap words in velvet to illuminate
Or be the unchecked tongue that stabs and brings to silence

Silence if we could only understand
Can teach what words can never say
The vibrations of words if we could only feel
Can break our fears and bring forth love

The tongue of every language
Conceived in words will always bring a change
Words well-spoken will move the biggest mountain
Or tear like thunder the very foundations of hope

But if all however in words allow saying
Is anchored in the wisdom of time we pass
Life, so simple with words to represent
Is worth the thought a bone to crack

JUSTICE

The Chief Law Officer went to town
To see for himself the adequacy of law
But there he saw bewildering:
Gangsters walking freely on the streets
Innocent men went with heads bowed down
For fear they may offend the hoodlums
The law has suffered blows
Public officers live in high places
The masses languish in the ghetto
Big rogues have become powerful
The masses remain paupers
They stew in their stinking squalor
They labour all day to ward off hunger
That yield only but a trifle
The children search desperately to find
That help has sunken with the evening sun
Justice has succumbed and become perverse
Survival is guaranteed
Only for those with smoking gun
And police brutalize their subjects
Who seek lawful protection
Bewildered by these observations
And underlined by no resistance
No one raised objection
The subjects all have chickened out
Bemused he wondered back to his office
He regretted as he wrote the obituary
Then hired a lively bull to rewrite the law.

WURA*

Gently whisper into my ears those words,
What love always means to you, I may have forgotten.

Gently cuddle me in your heart,
To discover those things I know not about love.

Gently raise my thoughts into the realm,
That my actions continually reflect love.

Gently reveal to me the beauty within you,
Which no man has ever seen before.

Gently settle into my heart like morning dew,
That I may blossom like roses do.

Gently call me to caution if I become selfish,
For such negates love in every way.

Gently show your large heart,
If I should act in an uncaring manner.

Strongly believe that I would reciprocate as well;
To keep open the door, through which we return the gift of life.

* Wura is a feminine name in the Yoruba language of Nigeria meaning, "precious one".

Adamu Ajunam

LOVE OR LEAVE HER

Staying here, tires me
Checking out, tires me
Keeping quiet, tires me
Talking more, tires me
The growing filth, tires me
Turning a blind eye, tires me
Going round problems, tires me
Shifting blames, tires me
No progress, tires me
Non-performers, tire me
Boot lickers, tire me
Sycophants, tire me
Law breakers, tire me
Bad enforcers, tire me
Joining them, tires me
Jungle justice, tires me
Justice denied, tires me
Sleepy compatriots, tire me
Crooked fellowmen, tire me
Playing along, tires me
Being frustrated, tires me
Loving her this way, tires me
Denying my love an empty lie
A bolt from the blues quiets me
Unbending resolve will break the jinx
Sowing a seed will bring hope
Nursing the plant will guarantee a future
Only true love will eclipse confusion

THE YORUBA DANCER

As the juju music her mind sedates
And the talking drum decodes the vibes
The felicity in her heart unfolds like a rose
She moves her legs smoothly into the flow
Dancing like the wings of a butterfly.

Turning her head blissfully like a peacock
She dangles her wrapper lustfully inviting
Gyrating easily like a perfect mixer
She lifts her head into the sky
And revels in the romance
Only music can give to the body.

Like gentle waves rolling over water
She graciously rotates her body
Shaking her hips to the melodious rhythm
The rigidity of her bones
Are all lost and gone
Carried away by the trick of the drum

Pretty Yoruba dancer I salute
The damsel with the glowing eyes
Gracefully twisting like a swan
Watching your steps evokes in me ecstasy
How late have I not been telling the world
To celebrate these footsteps only a child's play

Encore my damsel the ovation will continue unending
The wind will carry this rhythm beyond our coast
Where man will with open arms embrace
The warmth of the Yoruba dancer
Say it louder with the talking drum
Our cheering voices will never drown.

Adamu Ajunam

WHERE IS THE LOVE?

That lunatic we all know
Roaming the streets to no destination
Today lies forlorn and condemned
His hurting feet, slowed him down
When overwhelmed by fatigue
Abandoned to his fate, he lay
Like an unwanted rag
The multitude walked, surging past him
Baffled by how he is priced
I stood and watched.
Until a thought tumbled into my head
That he may have passed away
The fright of this thought
Sent a chill over my body
My heart became heavy
As I rewound his daily routine
He foraged from the dustbin
Poking and turning the garbage
Like scavengers do
To find some rot to feed upon.
Whether by rain or shine
The road was his home
With no clothes at all to cover his frame
Our cruel minds have failed us
We sentenced him by our neglect
We turned him into that animal
Like many to die uncared for
He lay motionless and stiff as stone
Only food for the droning flies.
The multitude filed past his remains
Not paying the last respect
Where is the love?

THE DECLINE

Little at a time
A haven is inching to a stop
Hope is sinking like the evening sun
The dimming lights foretell bondage
The small wounds are becoming cancerous.

Little at a time
Independence is losing value
The small gains are washing away
Anarchy is gaining foothold
Crude life is rolling back.

Little at a time
The system is becoming corrupt
The operators are losing their bearing
The stewards are becoming masters
Human right is becoming a nullity.

Little at a time
The gully is getting wider
Brotherhood is losing value
Poverty is becoming a lifestyle
Evil is becoming an acceptable norm.

Little at a time
Big trees are bowing out
Grass blades are dying
The offshoots are wilting away
Emptiness is becoming our portion.

Little at a time
Fear is becoming our companion
Distrust is devouring friendship
Great dreams are fizzling out
The bottom line is clear like sparkling water.

Adamu Ajunam

TO THE BIRD

Teach me how to sing, little bird
That my mouth may bring gladness like your whistling
Awaken me at dawn with your sonorous sound
That my look shall remain cheerful by day
As I wonder through this thicket full of struggles

Show me how you cover your skin
With your cloak of feathers
That my skin may grow downs
And pass through the wagging tongues
Not ruined by the plot of my enemies

Harbour me a little while in your nest
Little bird, that I may learn the wisdom
To emulate the openness and never fearing
Freed from the trappings of material riches
And protected by the armor coming from above

Let me fly only once the sky with you
Little bird, to catch just a glimpse
Of the view you constantly enjoy
To leave my worries for a while
I am happy to tell of another life.

MOMENTS

Birth, is only but a moment
The journey through life is full of moments
Moments never stop, they only pass a chasm
Returning with a veil for man to decode
Ugly Moments ache like load to the chest
Cherry moments lubricate like oil on rusting wheels
Moments always returns man to the potter's wheel
Moments long or even short

Moments come and go but their trails stay on
Like the path a whirlwind cuts in a moment's fury
A moment of shock or even blackout
Leaves a void that cannot be filled
Sad moments are unavoidable milestones
Coming like a thief in the middle of night
To steal our peace and leave us unstable
Moments long or even short

Another moment there is joyous moment
When misfortune for a moment have no place
A moment of success or dream comes true
Is an exciting elixir than a field of opium
And the spirit is hale like a bubble in the air
Merry moments make the foundation
On which hope is built and kept alive
Moments long or even short

All which forms man are encounters with moments
The trails that is left behind is the journey covered
All the moments not understood are as barren as the desert
Life's entire journey is a symphony we orchestrate
And the music propels the spirit between pain and joy
Moments of pain subdue the spirit
And merry moments keep hope alive
Moments long or even short.

Adamu Ajunam

MOONLIGHT NIGHT

Moonlight night, the golden face
That rises from the west
Your amorous eyes
Remain our beacon
Guiding us in this journey we make
Your distant smile
Reinforces our trust
To have sighted our destiny
Your tranquillizing glow
Is flowing down our veins
To replenish our minds
And refreshen the promise
We trust we shall drink of
As we walk to embrace the future
We are freed from the mental torture
We long succumbed to
The twinkling stars
Prophesy a new dawn
The shooting stars
Are good harbingers
As they swiftly pass the sky
Our thoughts soar higher
And our adrenalin in sympathy feels the same
We know we will reach the east
To meet the rising sun.

NWANNE

She comforted me when all I knew was sulking and sucking.
She was my fortress when I was afraid and helpless
She became my counsellor, when I outgrew her smacking,
I found in her a sibling, when I came of age,
Her loving admonition, is today my dyke

In these changing times, when the pace is jet set
Her listening ears still remains a source to rely
To lighten the load, a weary heart may carry,
In her heart is warmth that will thaw severe frigidity
And revive a sagging spirit that has suffered mischance.

Her love is like the freshness of spring,
And her sacrifices remind me to never derail.
The joy that I was initiated to cherish life as a gift,
Crowns the beauty, of the heart of Nwanne
Nwanne, my mother, my mentor.

Adamu Ajunam

BARGAINS

I

A friendly salute, accented with the charm of a rose,
A mouthful of questions aimed to court the mind,
A batter of thoughts to break the stands,
A little yield will ease the flow.
A persuasive debate may corner a compromise,
A word of wisdom let in between may flatter the heart,
An unguarded thought may prick like torn of a rose,
A good bargain fulfils both ends.
To bargain with patience may even the difference,
A soul in need may run short of.

II

If situations become gloomy like unclear weather,
If options become vague, in a world of choices,
If relations turn distressed and the thoughts are poisoned,
If love crosses the thin line to become hate,
If emotions boil and the lid is blown,
If rivalry turns to become a deadly affair,
If time turns slim and hope is yielding like a fallen tree
If life slides down the hill you never bargained
If a ray of thought strikes from a deep breath to offer redemption
You will be at liberty much freer than a circus clown.

III

We christen a new born baby to carry a unique identity,
By us a name that glorifies or mark an indelible experience,
A name reflecting hope or tall wishes preserve,
Influence is wealthier than riches,
Let us wait and see what God will do,
Whichever it may be, will remain like an indelible ink.
The craft of this decision come like the lobes of a kola nut,
The choice may be that of a counsel of kith and kin,
Or the privilege of a sage to chose and consecrate,
Whichever may be remains the sacred shadow,
A symbol of the manifold bargains we are all born to pass.

IV

When my eyes fell on the fairy I prayed to be my wife,
In her eyes I saw light that shone like from the galaxy,
Until my dreams come true, a time must pass,
To verify if my manhood will pass the test of my desire
If I only riches possess, my dreams will shatter like porcelain,
If I show ancestral wisdom, there is hope the knot will hold,
If I do not show meekness, cold winds will freeze my heart,
If I display genuine manhood, our hearts will sure unite,
If I wish to win my rose from her lineage,
I must bargain with the incorruptible prize of love.

V

When the naked sores which deface our cities disappear,
My heart will stretch to embrace the lilies that will grow,
My head I will bow to pray for the souls it claimed,
My rhymes will resurrect dead trees.
Many more shall live to ripeness beyond the biblical age,
Many more eyes shall see the beauty covered with overgrowth,
Many more lives shall refuse coexistence with poverty,
Many more minds shall grow as tall as the iroko tree,
These empty lines can in no way reflect my agony,
When the sore disappears our bliss will bubble like a perfect spring.

VI

If we must move to catch with time
Should we look up and focus like the eagle?
Should we be uptight like slaves confined in chains?
Should we unlock our all resources or trust only in destiny?
Should we be full of wits or exhausted like empty barrels?
Should we succumb to envy only compared to a livid liver?
Should we not act together like a harmonious choir?
To filter each option may earn us sweet nothing,
To turn back time a muse too costly to embrace
If we chose the duality of space and time to reach the mind,
We will celebrate the trinity of joy in our hearts as one.

ENJOY A COKE

Far way in the country of the Yankees,
Where skyscrapers tower high to reach the sky,
Where limousines are a symbol for better life,
Where hope and promise can be kept alive,
Where to be seen or heard,
Do not conflict with life existence,
Where hot dog is munched for the snack it is,
Where coca cola always graces the American dream,
Where it is served chilled like water in Alaska,
Where coke billboards have a place in the American mind,
The message fulfilled enjoy a coke,
The Yankee without a coke is a joke unimagined.

Back here in a tiny African village,
Where the people have no control over their tomorrow,
Where hope is a stranger like grass in the desert,
Where the huts so small, like the burrow of a rabbit,
Where great distances are covered only on foot,
Where staying alive remains a struggle,
Where a stint of dream is absent as well,
Where the cost of a hot dog would feed a chief's family,
Where to secure the meal for the day is at great peril,
Growing in this misery the demand for coke is alarming,
Their pennies gone for coke warmer than hot coffee,
The Yankees sold a culture with no dream to hold on.

Adamu Ajunam

THE REGRET OF MUNGO PARK

Dear Africa, the cradle of light
Your natural freedom captured my fancy
Controlling me like possessed to fulfill a dream
I proceeded like a greenhorn unto the sea
The wild and stormy sea roared in anger
And I laboured my conscience to ends
Why this dream so obsesses me.
Not even the yawning tide will swallow my urge.

My thoughts rocked feverishly
In sympathy with the turbulence
They wandered in the vastness
Of the open sea and found no support
Your protective hands realizing my plight,
Guided me like a mother,
And washed me off your Negro coast
To guide me anew your true foot path.

At our first encounter, you were shy
I stood motionless and dumb like a tree
The pearl from the heat glided like honey
On your face, to accent your uniqueness
As a sign of the adoration I felt in me,
I gave you the mirror carried on me,
The smile with which you replied my gesture,
Stilled my fears realizing my dream.

Red Earth and Other Poems

Unlimited you were in your freedom
As I was amazed at the wealth bestowed on you
Believe me my friends in Africa,
I told my folk of your beauty beyond compare
Many like me were awe-inspired
But the impatience and excitement
That overtook their desire
Plunged them into the scramble for Africa.

As my spirit continuously returns to your beautiful land,
I regret the mischief brought by the partitioning,
Although I find it difficult to reconcile,
That you still fail to recognize how tall you are,
In the jungle were the struggle is fiercest,
The iroko stands and will not give up her height,
My heart bleeds for the opportunities lost,
My eyes behold hope that will never fade.

Adamu Ajunam

THIS GENERATION

They are only infants and sprouting, just children
Needing all warmth to stand tall
Their minds still fragile like the butterfly
They must still feed from the milk of human kindness
Many yet so tender are coerced to carry their fate,
Staggering with a burden no child can bear.
They are only children but growing into a misguided generation.

They are under five years old, just children
They climb the ropes aping the jungle we offer them.
We purge love from their hearts
And teach them the art of the dark ages past
We culture them to believe they must be bulls in China shop
We concern ourselves not a shade and poison their minds,
They are only children but growing into a misguided generation.

They are under ten years old, just children
We show them naked power
More deadly than high voltage power.
Gun-shooting law enforcers that willfully maim
Horse whipping uniformed men
Who strip fellow citizens of every right.
They are only children but growing into a misguided generation.

They are teenagers, just children
We expose them to unbridled corruption
To levels that rob his brother the right to live
Abuse of office is courted like a beautiful bride,
Public servants metamorphose into tin gods
And precious values have decayed leaving cankerworms
They are only children but growing into a misguided generation.

They are juvenile not yet responsible, just children
Their ideas are like clay in the potter's wheel.
We accept lawlessness and stir the bee's hornet,
The result is chaos that burns life like a candle.
We have lost touch with a priceless culture,
To be your brother's keeper ensures love never dies
They are only children but growing into a misguided generation.

We now fostering, were once like them, just children
We enjoyed the milk of kindness; wisdom must flow in our veins
If the signs ahead don't rattle us,
The miles ahead are laid with mines.
We must pull the brake, if this train must not derail
They are just children, a helpless generation.
We owe them this, we owe them all.

Adamu Ajunam

THE NEXT GENERATION

The future generation is up and next
Though scarce like pin in a stack of hay
Their presence is assured like the sun in the sky.

The generation of today wears a mournful face
Knowing not the tonic and comfort a smile can bear
They roast in the anger that is fanned by frustration.

The future generation is like a gem in a pack
They are pure like gold and cannot be corrupt.
They know there is a tomorrow that begins today.

The generation of today absorb with the speed of snail
They will not yield even to the slave driver's whip
And even weeping a bucket is an action so futile.

The future generation is not like donkeys
A thousand words is conveyed with a wink of an eye
And brotherhood, whether east or west, flows from the heart.

The generation of today is scared of any challenge
They accept common place as if to say eureka
And admire haste as though it was noble.

The future generation shows the courage of a lion
Never retreating from the mountain that remains unconquered
And drink from the cup of success long lasting life experience

The generation of today is uncannily dubious
They remove the ladder from him that is climbing
They care less if the fall the roof may crash

The future generation is humane to his fellow man
They are quick to know the peril never to rock the boat
 Each for all and all for one to make a nation

LAGOS UNDER SIEGE

Lagos is in dire need to arrive at El Dorado
Three rivers separate her from berthing there:
Her people arriving in droves and overflowing her limits,
The deprivation her children suffer that turns them to be urchins,
The greed of few who cornered the cow that spends the milk,
Lagos is a beautiful city flawed by forces that bring decay.

Adamu Ajunam

OUR DIFFERENT LEADERS

They spoke so eloquently to win our freedom
We trusted them blindly they took us for a ride
Their thoughts ran riot and time ran out
They were soon booted out we welcomed the change.

They claimed vision that will remove our yoke
We voted them in but they squandered our tomorrow
We were overcome by darkness, we turned wretched
They were soon booted out we welcomed the change.

They were soldiers usurping power with guns and horsewhip
We were frightened to the marrow which gladdened their hearts
They soon fell into a slumber and forgot their mission
They were soon booted out we welcomed the change.

The army mutinied within and mauled the bond
The value for life not worth more than a chicken
They plucked a dozen innocent and walked away freely
They were soon booted out we welcomed the change.

They claim to lead us forward but we end up backwards
Our collective hope has shattered like broken china
Another messiah from the blues will rise and gain appeal
And his unsteady steps will see him out, we will welcome the change.

THE THIRD WORLD

Pardon the mind bogglers who make theories that scale nations
I see Africa miserable in all your forecasts and I wonder
Forgive the thinkers who see crystal ball where foam bubbles exist
Those great in oratory but forget the common man is still the issue.

Everywhere I go, I hear them speak a third world exists
My apologies, UN is the new world order a forgone conclusion.
Deprivation has turned a tool to deflate the ego of the poor,
Pardon me, if I still believe God created all to be equal.

With due respect, I know America is a great nation
My apologies to history, the Greeks if you remember did see it all.
Forgive me, if I mention Egypt was not less in greatness
Africa was the beginning and will not be the end.

My apologies to every African hounded and has developed cold feet.
The light that removed the curtain of darkness shone first in Egypt
That freed the thoughts to fly in the mettle of the eagle.
Pardon me, if I sound boastful but the nature of truth is transparent

Excuse me if I look into the future to register the new world order
Excuse me if I simply forecast, there can be no progress without equality
Pardon me, if I introduce a simple thought on the brotherhood of man
If I recall the teachings of great minds, only love can save us all.

Adamu Ajunam

BEAUTIFUL NUBIA*

We are Nubians the cradle of Africa,
We come from the land where the sun rises from the earth
Our mien is filled with warmth where mortals freeze for shock
We are not broken albeit the hefty burden on our heads

We are marching across nations to greet our brothers,
We shall circle the continent with joy in our bosom,
To see the offshoots of the seeds of Nubia
We shall free the seeds that fell amid sharp thorns

We are sailing the Nile up to Alexandria,
To see the pyramids which remain awe-inspiring,
We shall traverse the desert in our vessel of brotherhood,
Watching the glory of sunset on the expanse of the desert

We shall stop at Timbuktu to honour the nobles,
Who saw wealth beyond the limits of the worth of gold
And pray to the Almighty at the holy place in Jenne,
We are from Nubia and ask for peace in Africa

We are climbing atop the Kilimanjaro,
To see if any soul may still be in bondage across the land,
We shall descend from here to the great Zululand,
To salute the courage of the celebrated Madiba

We are marching from north down to the south,
We shall visit Cape Town to greet our freed brothers,
We shall open the bowels of the earth
To flush out any spirit that feeds on the creed of prejudice

*Nubia is the homeland of Africa's earliest black culture with a history going back 5,000 years in time.

UNTIMELY DEATH

Everyday is a gift of grace,
When we are fit to run the race,
That will end at a time,
When every soul shall breast the tape,
Living the worries to run no more
The grace to run is guaranteed,
By Him that is almighty.
Our hats are thrown into the arena
To battle for our needs and we perfect the art
To defend our existence braver than a lion
We peak at maturity and may win laurels
Only to walk unto old age as we keep faith.
Joy and pain are landmarks never forgotten,
Three scores and ten is hoped for all
But there is a wicked messenger,
Taking advantage of the pitfalls
Our indifference place on the track
Patiently waiting to pluck life untimely,
Death remains the deathless one
Untimely death cruelly stops the clock
Of many not mature to kick the bucket
Bowing out still young and promising
And make the headlines that break the heart
Why do we allow mountains of garbage to grow
That make nuisance of sight and health
To creep as enemies with unseen hands into the temples
Giving room to untimely death
To strangle the young at heart
Why do we reason with hate
At the differences in our tongues

Adamu Ajunam

Stirring chaos and confusion
Giving room to untimely death
To consume the bones yet to mature
Why do we not descend on the bandits?
Who strike even at those that have no neat penny.
Why do we allow the carnage?
That lies as undesirable street ornament
On which dear ones stumble to depart prematurely.
Why do we lick the venom politicians' vomit?
That cause affect and stifle the mind
Hailing destruction and untimely death?
Why do we still pretend, we have nipped the bud?
When untimely death is still on the prowl?

MY SIN WITH TIME

I squandered time
And I now compare to a novice
I dissipated time like steam
Until my kettle ran dry
I fooled with time

I squandered time
And my well is shallow
I always had the pole position
But I chose the foolish path
I lavished time.

I squandered time
I never thought the sun will set
My bed was left like a battle field
Drunken with sleep I feel displaced
Standing at the edge I fear the fall

Adamu Ajunam

SHAKA THE ZULU*

Judge me not dear friend
With the yardstick of an unfriendly soldier
Or the foolhardiness of a youthful bull
My heart only beckons that you may join
To free from the yoke of mental slavery
And reach for the sky with no frontiers
We must fly and never be caged
And touch the dreams to our hearts fulfillment

Come all you friends of Zululand
Bring your freed wills as only weapons
Come and buy into the wisdom of the ants
Working in piecemeal to create an anthill
I gave you Mandela to learn forgiveness
Never compromising the dream an inch on the way
Good dreams are worth sacrifice, no matter the odds
Duplicate the dreams in every heart that they remember.

We will lie in ambush, the grass of home cuddling our hearts
We will receive the spirit to convert the hypocrites
We will give strength to those who stand aloof
To swell our numbers and strengthen our cause
Again I remind you of another warrior to emulate
Martin Luther King, of blessed memory
He conquered his foes with no spear or shield
The power of his dream broke for his people a fatal jinx.

*Shaka the Zulu ruled Zululand in the 18th century. He turned Zulu tribe from a clan to a nation that held sway over a great portion of South Africa.

LAGOS LIFE

Lagos life is pivoted on a fragile scale
Swaying unevenly in search of a balance
And impatience is uncharitable to those without
To charge like a bull is not the Lagos acumen.

Lagos life, like glowing fire, is hot
Smoldering gently, burning frail nerves
The heat consumes the naïve
And the weak drown in a waiting sea of woes.

Lagos life pulsates with her peculiar rhythm
The heart is cheered when reason can thrive
A senseless event often buckles the mind
For in Lagos no act is considered impossible.

Lagos life can feign to be a teacher
The products that absorb this delusion
Never transcends the circle of selfishness
Perfecting in double talk or tongue is Lagos sense.

Lagos life imbibes the conscience of class
Where the river widens everyday between rich and poor
Survival here is war respecting no truce
The decay is festering deeper, the qualm more menacing.

Lagos life is laced with coded wisdom
Native wisdom obtained only on the streets
Lagos life can fool even the wise
Who unwittingly may hold unto a worthless glimmer.

POVERTY

Kick out poverty
Before it overtakes us
The cries of mothers who suffer this fate
Is becoming increasingly upsetting
Fathers battle daily to weather the storm
The children blinded by despair turn to crime
Those who lost all hope become monsters
Kick out poverty - it dehumanizes;
In any form – before it overtakes us
Poverty wears the face of misery and defeat,
And her claws deflate the hope to survive.
The dignity of man that walks this path
Is shattered and lamed to remain only vegetable
Kick out poverty, it dehumanizes;
Kick out poverty – before it overtakes us.

VIP ROAD CLOSURE

The heart of the city is gripped with fear
Everyone must stand still the VIP is on the lose
The VIP on a routine journey will ride
On the backs of tax payers who remain passive
What it costs her people, no one will ever count
The VIP by duty, is the people's servant
There is an unpleasant calm,
And frenzy his escort cannot do without,
For the VIP to make his flight
The guards are irritated by anything that moves,
The coast is cleared for the bull on the run,
So dictates the ordinance to keep him secured
The safety of his people, the least he cares,
Who buy reinforced doors to make secure,
But the iron gates fall like the walls of Jericho
When the hoodlums come marauding
The VIP may arrive long hours after the closure
The crowd waits patiently licking their wounds
The sirens hoot and blare to drown the anger
Be calm, be calm it seems to hoot,
Glittering limousines announce the servant,
The roaring sirens drown all conversations
The motorcade flies into another world
And after which the curtain drops
Emptiness and vanity trails behind
Dejection and apathy are not left in the turmoil
As the VIP disappears into another world
Wailing voices are left in the surging crowd,
Too late, the VIP has made his flight
This hubbub he never gets to hear.

Adamu Ajunam

THE NIGERIAN FACTOR

The Nigerian factor is not the anointed oil
That will remove the frosty relations that hinder unity
It is not the silver lining we crave for
It is not the fresh garden soil
Upon which universal love will grow
Or keep alive our strength and resilience
For which we as a people are known.

The Nigerian factor is like a grain of sand
Lodging between the wheel of time
It is like the fouled thought that easily dispels the crowd
It is like viewing the world from the window of a prison cell
It is a clog that jams the flow
It is like throwing stone in the market place
It is like vultures fighting over carcass
It is like the greed that separates the wolf from the herd.

The Nigerian factor is not the absence of will
That is inevitable to build a great nation
It is not denying the truth
That we wish to remain our brothers' keeper
Only the supreme sacrifice very little volunteered
It is the permutations we overstate
That erodes success from our very eye
It is the gamble to pull each other down

The Nigerian factor is like a wedge
Driven between the heart of a people
It is like the straw that breaks the back of the camel
Frustrating little success that take a life time effort
It is the gloating of the fool who thwarts the wish of the people
It is the lack of patience that stirs chaos
It is the lack of decorum covered by pitiful vanity
That places the infamous crown; her people never deserve.

THE LOST SMILE

The rose that loses its charm and withers away
The heart of the mother Africa bleeding
For the bleak days ravaged by hatred
For her children who turn child soldiers
For her children who will never know peace

She is mourning her children claimed by wars
She is weeping for the land covered by blood
She is mourning her children maimed by hunger
She is imprisoned by darkness that suffocates hope
She knows no other taste but the bitter pill of life
She is sorrow-stricken and has lost her smile.

She can no longer cry or blood will flow
She can act no otherwise but to walk away from sorrow
She must elevate her mind to wear the tears of joy
The smile of Buddha will be etched on her lips
The flood of harvest ending the drought

Her face will glow like chrysanthemum
The glint of light in darkness will bring hope
The thought of a new day will cuddle her heart
The quiet of a still lake will bring her peace
The dawn, I pray, will embrace her tomorrow
A caged bird that sees a chance and flies into freedom

Adamu Ajunam

AFTER THE BOOM

As soon as the black gold emerged
Pumping from the depth below their feet
Their heart soared high to reach the sky
Their eyes widened to settle for all that glitters
The values shifted to embrace all that is greed
And illusion became the cornerstone of living
The visions got blurred and faded away
Wild dreams sprouted faster than mushrooms grow
They cared less to learn the ropes they climbed
That tomorrow like a candle is easily spent
The boom triggered insatiable appetite
That consumed the grains of reasoning
But the boom, like a bird in a maiden flight
Came tumbling and plummeted to the floor
Reducing would-be linchpins to little pawns
A free and fierce fall seized the nose in the mud
The agonies of the pains they never end
The coma has left a trail of sorrows
Tomorrow has turned uncertain with the clouds above
Values have decayed and turned to rags
Anarchy festering like cankerworm
The droning of the emptiness is deafening
The boom that came to wipe their tears
Turned the albatross they pray forever surrender.

TO BE BORN TODAY

I can not divine in the feeblest manner
Why yesterday still so obsesses me
It can not be the crave only to fathom
Why my forbearers drank from a well of love
Or to deny that I still suffer like a caged bird
And remain unable to savour liberty.

I do not brood over the lost romance
With nature, in the African jungle now decapitated
I savour the memory of our fathers as truly freed
Not the clichés about freedom that dwarf my spirit today
And the mental poison that ties me with in chains
I crave to draw strength and soar like an eagle.

I shall not dwell on the thoughts of the good old yesterday
Luxuries today are plenty and teasing
I am drilled to see the smile they took away from me
To be born here today in this labyrinth
When hollowed minds become easily immortalized
Constantly taking us back like bulls engaged in head butting.

It is not the shame to be branded as a lost generation
That leaves me wailing my crocodile tears
We are sharp to recognize who is not our tribe
Not for the sake of succour but to destroy with the arrow of hate
Many have become chatterers unable to hear the humming dove
Preferring to tread the path where victory lays a broken mirror.

I will rather let yesterday be a distant past
And beckon on the spirits to heal the wounds
To find the key we lost in our battle of hate
And rekindle the night into a mirthful day
That we born today in this very criss cross
Bear the worthy intention to unmask all veiled slavery.

Adamu Ajunam

THE MOBILE TAILOR

Obioma* is the tailor
Elongating the life of rags
To cover the shame of the poor
Who will never wear new linen
With his yarn of hope and nimble hands
He patches the soul of the rags
Weaving and close netting like a spider web,
He is ever popular with the wretched
Wherever they may find abode,
He roams the street like a sleep walker,
With his junk and trite device
Padded on his head or sunken shoulder
Cocking his ears with rapt attention
He hopes to hear a distress call.
Obioma is the small-time tailor
His commitment is rewarded only in tokens.
He patches rags of many colours
To cover the nakedness of the down trodden
He cuts and mends their different tatters,
To fit their meager frames,
Those are never so concerned with what is in vogue.
Whether over size or second hand,
Condemned from foreign land,
Obioma has the answer
He brings smile to the deprived.
His dreams are not too high, only to stay alive
His soles are hardened and full of corns
Trekking like a donkey unenviable mileage
He is not an enemy of government
Even if he never pays his taxes

Many more like him are daily wasted
Believing the state will one day change heart
Many lives will continually be wasted,
Like that obioma who patiently waits until that day
When Death shall remove the pains
He lives one day that grace will come his way

*Obioma means "good heart" in Ibo language, now generally accepted as a name for the small-time tailor who roams the streets with his worn-out sewing machine in search of livelihood.

Adamu Ajunam

SOCIAL SECURITY

The pocket calculator is a brain box
Grinding numbers like a mow machine
Churning out answers that will not calm the hopeless
Its brain is faster than sound but lacks a human face
Chewing numbers, no matter how stout the volume may be
I need a calculator monthly, to give me a human face
And help me share my penny
I punch my obligations into this brain
To tell me what's left for me
I have foremost a family
To whom I owe the most
I am my brother's keeper
I dare not forget to key in
There are my kith and kin
Not dispatched empty handed
Then followed by a queue defiled
By our social insecurity
That no meek heart will look away
There are the aged and lonely ones
Waiting to pick manna
That falls from benevolent hands
The wayside is filled with the handicapped
Whose plight evokes pity
There are the down-trodden million
Who cannot determine their future
If not helped with a widow's mite
No matter how I stretched my penny
It never covered my heart's desire
I summed it all with one apology
Praying no social guilt ever weighs me down
For them my penny will never cover
In our insecure land

THE DAY OF CREATION

If you a moment perfect silence could achieve
If you a while like a still lake could wait
If you the fears of silence could overcome
If you now the travails of the universe could behold.

If you a moment your eyes could shut
If you the bountiful blessings of the world could behold
If you the denials and misery of the poor could compare
If you took to heart you might feel the hurting.

If you a while with attention could listen
If you are not deceived by the hypocrisies of equality
If the helplessness of many would not make you cry
If the inhumanity would not bring you down your knees

If you could now one deep breath inhale
If you could now arrest all your thoughts
If you could place yourself inside the suffering
If you would promptly let this burden go

If the burden would stir you to act and bring some smile
If your resolve to change would remain consistent
If your crusade only with love would pursue
If you loathe violence as weapon and would achieve.

You walk into the embrace, the new day of creation.
The day when tolerance would reign supreme
The day that all hearts would know no darkness
The day all would stand on a pedestal justice to hold.

Adamu Ajunam

LOVE THEME

Lilies may be pure, roses may charm
The freshness of the blossom may enchant the air
Love is more and like wine that fools the heart,

The luster of diamond may shine in the dark
The magic of gold may alter fortunes
Love is more and a gush of it can flip the mind

The bolt of lightning may tear the sky
The rays of the sun is laden with potent
Love is more and trifle dose can swirl the spirit.

The horn of the snail are filled with senses
 Chicken have a field day when hawks are absent
Love is more and a quantum in the heart helps overcome

Love is like the smile radiating from the sun
Love can be pain turning into gain
For those who chose to suffer patiently

Love is like the warmth, flowing in the blood
That can turn a jelly mind into a fearless lion
Love can turn the unrepentant to be a beacon of light

Love is like a gate that leads to a treasure
Love can be the biggest prize for those who find
Love is the highest school that has no coach.

REQUIEM

A light that burns in the open field
At a time of the day when all is dark
In the dark of the night covered by tall grasses

A light that burns when the air is still
In the dark of the night when all spirits must journey
At a time of the night when fear grips the air

A light that is flickering in the heart of the night
In the dark of the night and cannot shine in the dark
At a time of the night when light must shine

A light that smolders without hope to rekindle
At the time of the night when praying fails and hope flees
In the dark of the night when the body is stiff

A light will die in the open field when the air is still
In the dark of the night when tall grasses cover the night
At a time of the night when hope flees and the body is stiff

Adamu Ajunam

THE GARDEN

Come with me to see a garden,
Where plants thrive but refuse to bud,
The garden exists only as pasture for lost sheep.

Tell me another story,
No man survives from eating flowers.

The garden with time increased and grew,
Receiving all the care nurseries get but remained drab,
Like a nation suffering stagnation.

Tell me another story
No man survives from eating flowers

There were times it looked like budding,
But ravaged by animals or aborted by ants,
Like an ulcer that never heals and pains forever.

Tell me another story
No man survives from eating flowers

Man must not eat flowers to survive and grow,
Blending our strength expands us like the Baobab tree
Dwelling on our weakness will stifle our consciousness.

Tell me another story
No man survives from eating flowers.

White and red flowers can thrive together,
Yellow and blue flowers do not destroy the beauty,
Living in harmony is the beauty of the symphony of life.

SALUTE TO QUEEN NZINGA*

They removed her crown and showered mock praises,
They shattered her heart and offered fake friendship,
They removed her peace and imagined her defeated,
They beheaded Ndogo grass and asked for treaties,
They looted her throne and flattered her ego,
The forgot the bullish strength, bestowed on Ndogo men,
They christened her Dona Anna,
And believed her resistance crumbled.

She remains the Queen Nzinga Mbandi,
No dark clouds or cannon will ever remove
Her native land and only love, her precious treasure
Life is desolate, without a home to lie,
When freedom is stolen, life becomes a prison.
Thought will grope like a lost sheep ever missing home.
Fear and misery will consume the heart,
We stand like rock to defend our freedom.

*Nzinga Mbandi, Queen of Angola in the 16th century. She brought together the tribes in Angola to fight the Portuguese.

Adamu Ajunam

JOGGING RHYME

Run, run jogger run.
Fire the lungs and don't be late
In and out, hold steady the pace
Down the route that is healthy and gay.

Run, run, jogger run.
Thrust your body into the wind
Let your pores open and skin breathe
As vital nutrients reach the blood

Run, run, jogger run.
Exhort idleness and strengthen the will
Removing the odds that may obstruct the mind
And renew life with loaded enthuse.

Run, run, jogger run.
Stir the thoughts that lie and wait
Mix them up with unfinished meditations
While you cruise and drop the worries

Run, run, jogger run.
Liven the soul with cosmic energy
When the body begins to bow from burden of weight
Lace the trainers and run again.

PEACE

Hurry only to understand
That haste attracts confusion
And the whirl thereof the spirit upsets.
Do not chase time like a dog after its shadow
Wasting away the beauty of life
Go stealthily
Through the unrest of this world
Seeking all wisdom
To bring you to the threshold
And join the spirit of those assured
Peace in eternity
Cherish the temple that dwells within
It is more rewarding,
Than the vexation inherent
When we run after time lost.
Stir not the spirit but remain steadfast
There are troubled waters we must swim,
There are defeats no one can forestall
Let none of these humiliate the spirit.
When alleys are closed
New windows must open
Hurry only to understand
That haste attracts confusion
Listen to the voice that has purpose but not intrusive
And will never surrender before a thousand army
A voice that even the deaf will hear
Impacting on life what only grace can bring
Hurry to understand
There is infinite power
In the voice that speaks within.

Adamu Ajunam

CITY EXPLOSION

They overtook the city in large numbers
It protracted grudgingly in ominous silence,
Abandoning the villages where grass welcomes home
Into the city where wolves abound and pitfalls are deep

Paradise they hoped in the city awaited,
Where all is in abundance and dreams fulfilled with ease.
Away from the narrow foot-tracks shared with ants,
Arriving into mansions where sleep is sweet.

In the city a strange emptiness embraced them all,
The many faces that throng the streets without an ear that listens,
Everyone engaged in the gruesome battle to survive,
Where brotherhood is doomed and love is not so dear.

When hope is shattered some turn to be plunderers,
Many faces are sorrow stricken for the wolves encountered
And victims falling daily from the tricks of knaves
Friendship built on face value never heals any wound.

Hope disappears like walking on quicksand
Many resign their fate to seek in the jail
Some bewitched by the nakedness they meet as company
The brave are undeterred by the height of the ghetto fence

The city outgrew her skin is poised to rupture,
The burden outlandish for her knees withstand,
The weak buried daily under the woes and find no solace,
Are wasted and churned in the mill of the city.

The fate of a city overflowing in numbers,
Is horror and pain for the helpless falling like geese
The face of a city ballooned and fettered with poverty
Is ugly, a sore to behold that finds no cure.

MAY

When May returns, we welcome
The month that beauty blooms,
The youth of the year come alive;
The withered fields abandon the rusty look,
To usher pastures return and greet the grass of home
The grey and dusty sky recedes,
For the deep blue of the ocean shines unto the sky.

May does crawl in,
With the speed of a beetle,
Bringing with her,
The precious gifts of nature,
The showers of the season,
It prompts the mind to sow seeds of hope,
It stimulates the heart with only thoughts.

May as a month,
Is awe-inspiring,
When nature paints her landscape;
Pictures so divine to lift the spirit,
When sunrise glows like molten iron,
And the morning dew is ever inviting,
We witness with joy the symphony of life.

When May arrives and the sun sets,
Life equates like a fragile embryo,
About to be born again;
To smell the earth and the grasses green,
It unfolds the mystery within the sphere,
May is like an oracle,
Foretelling the origin of the life we seek.

DECADENCE

Do you know that –
The idler today is most admired?
Working hard is unnecessary stress?
To be self-centred outshines team spirit?
Behaving well is obsolete manners?
Love without cheating is no longer fashionable?
Worrying about nature is only day-dreaming?
The toothbrush smile opens doors?
Being conspicuous is more appealing?
Asking questions is despicable manners?
Being considerate is for the feeble-hearted?
You need no brains to be accomplished?
To be hypocritical is an acceptable norm?
Brutality removes life hurdles?
And even murder is no longer abhorred?
Telling lies catapults you up?
Pulling down honesty has become unavoidable?
Hanging out with boot lickers will boost the ego?
Instant fame has become so attractive?
Rising at all cost is more exciting?
Crashing values is no more news?
Gate crashers have become heroes?
The more the table turns the more the decadence
The poorer it gets the lower the levels
The tread that sews us despite the status
Dovetails each spirit without a seam
The stiffness by which they refuse to change
Prolongs the journey and the cross we bear.

GO SLOW

When an excursion changes, turning into ordeal
And the grotesque journey ruffles the mind
When sightseeing turns wearisome and one is blinded by anger
When vehicles are so stressed that they totter or give up the ghost.

Go slow is the Lagos name for traffic frustration
Some traffic blunder not amicably settled
May be overturned to arguments or even a jungle rumble
Bringing traffic to an unbearable standstill.

Some drivers get mad and are ready for dog fights
Charging any opposition and becoming obscene
Car bumpers lock horns as they struggle for space
The emissions discharged make all uneasy.

The man-hour here squandered, would save a million lives
Trapped in the tumult those in the rear can never explain
They are hostages roasting in the heat of passing anger
Their tempers are tickled and verbal missiles do fly.

Very soon hawkers emerge the foot-soldiers they are
Desperate to win a penny for their belly
They sprint like gazelles to make a living
Not fearing the dangers in this avalanche of steel.

The resources wasted in a go-slow to mention a tip
The youthful energies both misapplied and untapped
The carpet of garbage they leave when the traffic dissipates
Thwart the dawn of any golden era one may secretly seek

Adamu Ajunam

Our leaders use go-slow as model for governance
Children are dying of hunger and starvation they only investigate
The youths have become militants, politicians exploit their poverty
For the aged who lack, the authorities call for a symposium.

POWER TUSSLE

Power, ever so transient ever so attractive
When the struggle is in the court we vie for it
When the court becomes a ring we fight for it
When the ring turns to battle field we buy guns
When death comes in the face we re-strategize.

Power, ever so transient ever so attractive
The old hold fast the young are in dire need to taste
The old think like foxes the young charge like bulls
When the door is narrowed we change to chameleon
The use for power a futile question only patience answers.

Power, ever so transient ever so attractive
A game ever so old not wished away
When the ring turns to battle field we buy guns
When the door is narrowed we change to chameleon
We forget all about love for little mischief.

Adamu Ajunam

ABUJA

Abuja has changed forever
From an unknown village in the hinterland
To a geographical nucleus
That will hold the spirits together
Into a city of the future and common destiny
The virgin land has been prodded
And the calm forfeited
The grass has withered from trampling
The foot paths have turned to highway
The rocks that offered hiding places
Have tumbled to the power of dynamite
To build bridges to the heart of the people
And the country that yearns for peace
Abuja has changed to become a beacon
Of hope to heal the wounds
Inflicted from the war of yesterday
And washed away the barricade
We often saw as tribe.
Standing on the crest of Aso Rock
I see the ancient city of Sokoto
Celebrating the life of Awolowo
The visions of Sardauna
Have become building stone in the Niger Delta
The large heart of Azikiwe is heralded in Kano city
Lagos will not give up the struggle
To reincarnate a dignified hub.
Abuja has become a centre
That will lead us into new ways of life
The grandeur of thoughts from the people's parliament

Shall usher in the long awaited freedom
The mansions in the city that glow and glitter
Will no longer allow for bad and dirty ways
Lagos must take the lead to graduate again
And re-establish her tropical beauty
Positioning as a city rich in aquatic splendor
Port Harcourt our garden city
Will boom again as a garden of paradise
The prize we must pay to nurture Abuja,
Will solve the riddle of our unity we left in doubt.

STALEMATE

Here we are devouring the love in our hearts
Cursing ourselves, our tribes and even clans
How can we survive and make the move?
We remain victims of our foes and give them joy.

Cursing ourselves, our tribes and even clans
We are overtaken by hunger and starvation
We remain victims of our foes and give them joy
The road to freedom is blocked with hurdles.

We are overtaken by hunger and starvation
Our throats are inflamed and desires to be quenched
The road to freedom is blocked with hurdles
The will of man on this path can be maimed.

Our throats inflamed and desires to be quenched
Our hopes are beclouded by a sudden smoke
The will of man on this path can be maimed
How long shall we wait to bear the yoke?

Our hopes are beclouded by a sudden smoke
How can we survive and make the move?
How long shall we wait to bear the yoke?
Here we are devouring the love in our hearts.

OUR BURDEN

Our necks have become long like ostrich
Stretching in expectation to see the coming of a new life
Our masters promised and we trusted gullibly as newly freed
Highlife is the name of this new life we still await.

Our leaders took mantle when baton changed
They promised a rosy bed from the squalor we lay
They repeated the promise until it sounded like a broken record
They too failed woefully they were only villains.

Baton changed continually our burden enlarged like hot balloon
The power of authority made them drunk and act like bulls
Leaving moral bankruptcy and total decay as only legacy
They looted the treasury with impunity, a sign post for mediocrity.

The military with their guns evicted the mercenaries
Turning the nation into a cantonment
No man uniformed dared to question
They fast tracked us to doom with such alacrity

Our ears overflow with warped lamentations
Why this journey has turned to a torture
The signs we see as we toil along is crystal clear
Are only poverty and suffering that knows no tribe

We are a rich people become impoverished
Seeding leadership, our birth right poorly lavished
The burden of indifference and the distrust we share
Tie our hands as the grace for greatness melts away.

Adamu Ajunam

THE VOICE IN THE WIND

The voice in the wind
Is the wave of the ocean pounding on the shore
It is the rustling of the river
Gathering from the creeks and brooks
It is the shine of the moon on a still lake.

The voice in the wind
Is not the sorrowing of the widow who lost her rights
It is not the sadness of a free born declared an outcast
It is not the mourning of a mother who lost her only child
It is not the pain of the etching of poverty on many faces.

The voice in the wind
Is vibrant like the sun that shines on my native land
It is clear like the shadow behind the sun
It is the good will bestowed from above
It is the weight that is lifted when our sufferings end.

The voice in the wind
Is the murmuring in our hearts we choose to ignore
It is the scars left when the storm shows its ugliness
It is the grace we seek when we feel abandoned
It is the longing for love to fill our emptiness

The voice in the wind
Is the the persona we grow when we go our way
It is the grace we get when we listen within
It is the endearing experience we reflect upon
It is the "thank you" muttered when we are alone

The voice in the mind
Is not garrulous to the secrets we entrust it
It does not roar like a lion to find acceptance
It is the voice we seek when searching for the golden advice
For in the end the answer is always blowing in the wind.

QUICK MONEY

Swindlers deadlier than swine they are
In love with money than shylocks compare
They warehouse their conscience will transverse any path
Bringing tears and sorrow to any home they visit
They come with charm but charlatans they are
Or bury their fangs in the glint of a grin
The mines they lay blow gullible hearts away

Some officials in authority are silent killers too
Mutilating papers that undo the rest
The power of their pens quicker than shot guns of the mafia
Signing away tomorrow and the children to slavery
Enriching their pockets faster than the speed of shooting star

For others these ways are too refined
They carry guns and knives and murder very cold
Brutally squandering lives of children yet to come to prime
As lambs of sacrifice to appease some god
Equating life not more than a mere housefly
Only to fleece wealth that dries up in the minute.

Adamu Ajunam

TRIBUTE TO PHILIP EMEAGWALI

You are the man
Growing taller beyond giants
To reach the height of the iroko tree
Your sweat has turned the river
Upon which the virtual world can navigate
And strangers meet in camaraderie
Not feeling the privacy invaded
Your labour has linked the global jungle
We cover distances with the world in our finger tips
If you were still at home
What would you have become?
Would you still be a star?
Some men are born
To journey into the wilderness
Conquering hopelessness to deliver dignity
Some hope become a beacon
Guiding humanity on the path
The glitter you shine today
Epitomizing glory for all black man
But you have turned a whiz-kid
Preying on the fruit of wisdom
You have learnt to fly
Not only by night alone
We now journey from Onitsha to Lagos
And even Lagos to Seattle
Measured like the flash of the mind
We owe this to your delicate net
And your mercuric mind refuses to slumber
Soaring outside our earthly realm
Hoping that your web
Will join all mankind with universal love
Your reasoning
To see a hundred years ahead
Makes you the lonely star
The captain of a ship linking planets apart.

DIVIDENDS OF DEMOCRACY

Politicians always speak with the tongue of a snake
Baking their cakes of plenty
In the ovens they fire with empty promises
They love the jamboree feeling but never a dissenting crowd
Even when underperforming, heaven remains an easy destination
Travelling in vessels fuelled only with borrowed time
Politicians are rare to find, who deliver honestly
No matter we see through them, we need to identify.

To be free like birds in the sky, we often crave to enjoy
But the constrains of nature confine our space
Our leaders steer the ship to help us fulfill God's will
To be our brothers' keeper we cannot ignore
Standing for the weak will remove the hell they suffer
Expanding the space will usher in freedom
Fighting for justice will bring about equality
Building bridges will join hearts together
Building brotherhood will shrink the world.

Blessed are the stewards who elevate the lives of masses
Politicians who fan embers remind us only of our differences
Dumping our democratic dividends into troubled waters
Turning their lust for power into our albatross
And our hope to excel is consumed by their heat of greed
In a world of plenty may our opportunities not be axed
We seek for men who honour the call in truth and humility
Looking beyond the ordinary, may be grace will intervene.

Adamu Ajunam

THE AFRICAN TIME

The African time is throbbing
From the heart of the infinite
Where all things come to be
It is ticking with the precision
Our enemies can not predict
It is echoing in the valley
Like the trumpet of the elephant
It is vibrating in the heart of the Africans
To consume all man-made barriers
It is gaining momentum
To arrive at the threshold
Where the clarion call
Will no longer fall on deaf ears
It will melt the heart of her enemies
Like Madiba forgave with the heart of gold
We shall catapult to new heights leap frogging
Africans will settle for nothing less
But only torchbearers of dignity
A new world of our own
In a world of possibilities
The African time
Is leaving behind her darkest hours
Fired by not only hope
But inspired by a new awakening
To catch with the rest
It has journeyed past the hills
That brought her frustration
It is tolling her bells
In synchrony with the mind of the giants
Our time will come and never be late.

MOLUE PALAVER

Molue is the clapped-out bus Lagos fell in love with
It does not get the care due a beast of burden
Judge it not with the spectacles of showroom cars
Some wobble for age but denied her rest in a Junkyard
Molue conductors are boorish and wear the claws of wolves
They easily tear a passenger who may run short of fares

The Molue at peak time is overstretched by duty obey
The weight of a million wayfarers a matter of daily routine
The predicaments of the Molue with time are over-flogged
The novice drivers escape jail for the law is porous
They are unpretending green horns in the art of cruising
Some drivers drink to be airy before they fuel their Molues.

Commuters suffer long patience awaiting the shanty bus
The scotching sun heats up their temper before the jerky ride
The Molue is aching from the blows buried under its ribs
If the Molue could speak, it would not halt at bus stops
Where they use any opening to enter for the ride
How can it stay decent with this awkward vulgarity?

Some drivers get derailed and act like hooligans too
They turn the road to a bar to talk about sweet nothing
Increasing the frustration the Molue suffers all
The Molue sometimes falls into an awful feat
Turning the road into a sick bay for long hours
To catch a routine check denied it by prolonged call to duty

The inside of the Molue can be set a stage for a circus show
A salesman in the belly offers trash to make a living
A preacher may break the silence to warn about Armageddon
All condoned by the conductor perching like a monkey
Caring for nobody's comfort never forgoes a dime
The Molue has aged and all wish a glorious exit.

Adamu Ajunam

ALL IS WELL

All is well when my heart is on fire – all is well.
It is well when the agony begins to motivate,
And the glow of success rekindles the spirit,
My mind follows the dictates of the voice within,
And my eyes see beyond the candescence of this fire.
My thoughts are chanelled to embrace peace and joy,
This interval I can not judge by any reason but do confess,
All is well when my heart is on fire – all is well.

SHADOWS IN THE NIGHT

When shadows grow taller beyond sunset – it is all dark
When the body finds a home under the earth – it is all dust
When good and evil meet one last time to part forever – are all dead
When shadows grow taller beyond sunset – it is all dark
The ears are attuned never to miss the call
To become initiated behind the curtain, what man still aches to know
When shadows grow taller beyond sunset – it is all dark
When the body finds a home under the earth – it is all dust.

Adamu Ajunam

THE SECRET OF EULOGY

The eulogist's verses
Are only kind words
That can wear off fear
The words of the verses
Like pin in a stack
May be hard to find
For those who drive with only whip.
The power of praise
When timely spoken
Can lift the spirit of man
That may only lie
Waiting for tide to wash away
Or stir the courage
Imprisoned by fear
To stand brave the sea
That need dictates at times to traverse
The words of praise
Must not be cynical
Some eulogy
When timely spoken
Will offer the keys
That opens otherwise impossible doors.

FOLLOW ME

Follow me with all your heart
Follow me even if I can not see beyond the hill
Stoke up the fire of love and promise me
The flame you ignite in me will never quench
You are to me what warmth is to fire.

Follow me love never dies
Follow me now that you trust in me
Tell me tales like in the beginning
Let me laugh and forget my fears
Lull me to sleep with your sonorous voice.

Follow me and fasten my hand
Follow me but lead the way
Bear in mind I falter like man
Not withstanding, love me now the way I am
We'll bury our shortcomings with goodwill flakes.

Follow me let us recount lovely memories
Follow me by day or night time never stops
Watch with me sunrise at the beach
Let us smelt our thoughts to be one
When you smile I feel secure.

Follow me the one that is mine
Follow me as we venture through life
Love is like larva with different stages
It begins with innocence that intoxicates the mind
And pass stages wilder than stormy waters.

Adamu Ajunam

Follow me even when you do not see me
Follow me you will feel love never dies
When I dial your sympathy line
My eyes bare the veil that covers the distance
You are so near when I kiss the air.

Follow me let us see eye to eye
Follow me as we stand in our nakedness
Nothing concealed, the same dreams we share
And pray that our ways have fused together
One more reason God must be our bedrock.

Follow me I will always stare at your smile
Follow me as our treasures grow and overspill
If ever in doubt return to our infancy
Fill the air with your unmistakable fragrance
When you smile I feel secure.

LOST OPPORTUNITY

The old man took
The only stone his treasure
He turned it round in fulfillment
It gladdened his heart
To know this jewel is worth a price.
Much more than just a head start
He dared not forfeit the stone
That shaped his life of peace
And polished by wisdom that made him the man
He saw a golden key
That unlocked many riddles
With the stone in his hand
It recalled the golden memories
If the jewel remained in his chest
His little boy he posed
Unarmed may wander misdirected
And become a game
For the wolves that loiter in the jungle
The jewel passed on as inheritance
To fulfill all righteousness a father owes.
Time went by
For this boy became man
He travelled down the road
To meet the twists and turns inevitable,
The stone abused and relegated
Was never a talisman
And spent his will on many wishes
Until he was consumed by idleness
Unable to redeem his manhood
He missed to learn the lessons
That man must always stand to be counted
The old man bemused and watched the space
As though he could turn back the hands of time
He recalled the jewel he esteemed
His eyes betrayed the bewilderment
How one nut got missing inside a little fire

Adamu Ajunam

RITUAL MURDERERS

Where are you going with the bloody hands
That felled the tree of life on which we all depend?

You fail to use the eyes of a lamb for thanksgiving
Those that portray innocence and meekness of heart
To fulfill the vows your lips have made
You pluck the eyes of a man and forever blind his fate.

Where are you going with the bloody hands
That felled the tree of life on which we all depend?

You fail to shoot the eagle in the sky
And inherit the bird's eye view your heart so desires
But remove the eyes of a man with limited vision
Who struggles to see with the mote in his eyes.

Where are you going with the bloody hands
That felled the tree of life on which we all depend?

You fail to fetch the head of an elephant
With a large vessel and dependable memory
But axe the tiny head of a little child
Who can barely recall his name.

Where are you going with the bloody hands
That felled the tree of life on which we all depend?

You fail to kill and acquire the powerful limbs of a lion
That possesses strong claws to choke its prey
But prefer to cut the limb of a poor old man
With a trembling hand that can not even lift a pin.

Where are you going with the bloody hands
That felled the tree of life on which we all depend?

ARMCHAIR CRITICS

The woman made a simple chair
A utility chair not an easy chair
A chair of gold she never wished
Not a throne intoxicates with power
Some chairs only turn to be hot seats
For those who fritter away grace to add value.
Her critics who never saw her limits
Bid chairs that would not soothe her pains.

Her lot was not a rocking chair
In her world with little windows
Where choices are even rarer
Than finding grass in the desert
Her choice remains a simple chair
To overcome the rudeness of poverty
Her critics who never saw her limits
Bid chairs that would not soothe her pains

An arm chair was available everywhere
Not fulfilling the dictates of her wish
She never asked to make a sofa
She wished no chair from the moon
A little chair of wood and nail
Only wide enough to survive a lowly servant.
Her critics who never saw her limits
Bid chairs that would not soothe her pains.

With the lowly life surround
The woman made a simple chair
As narrow to take her back
She leans to observe the world of plenty
Not the lavish chair that fits the noble
Who sits and taunts the spirit of the hapless
Her critics who never saw her limits
Bid chairs that would not soothe her pains.

Adamu Ajunam

THE PEOPLE'S PRAYER

Dear Lord, give us leaders
Who tower high above corruption
Who can gaze deep into the crystal ball
And behold not their image as self-centered bigots
But come with a heart of human kindness
To remove the web that deny his people joy.

Dear Lord, give us leaders
Who are truly tested and devoted servants
Who are not fatigued by the burden of a neighbour
To serve like bees without a single murmur
And savour the delight in lifting the sunken souls
Of those who have lost sense and purpose.

Dear Lord, give us leaders
Who do not speak from both ends of their mouth
Whose words will motivate dead grass to come alive
Invoking authority not to pervert justice
Whose mind are freed and not clouded by ethnic shade
And see their constituency as fatherland.

Dear Lord, give us leaders
Who shall lead beyond now to the land of glory
Where we stand tall not cowed by our peers
Keeping hope alive through all eternity
This prayer we say with a common voice
And we thank you with humility for granting us all.

HARMATTAN BLUES

When rivers dry and no longer chuckle
And the horizon is grey covered with a blanket of dust
When the weather cock looks only to the north east
Then you know that harmattan blues have filled the air.

When the sun shines like an unpolished ruby
And the heat no longer is oppressive
When moist is absent and the skin is coerced to whiten
Then you know that harmattan blues have filled the air.

When the lips are kept moist only by constant licking
And the earth so dry and the greenery wilt away
When all is dry and no waters from the heavens fall
Then you know that harmattan blues have filled the air.

When wild fires fan and the wild life live in fear
When the sun is numb and will no longer cheer
When the trees are naked and do not offend the pious
Then you know that harmattan blues have filled the air.

Adamu Ajunam

ZEALOTS IN THE MAINSTREAM

A drop of water
Is a gift of life
A thought of hate
Is taking life
The nectar in a flower
Is food for the ants
And a bouquet of flower
Is a message of love
The fragrance of a rose
Will excite the senses
The thought of God
Uplifts the soul
And a wicked thought
Will poison the mind
Purity and innocence
Are the hallmarks
Of the vision
Of true children
Kindness and warmth
Will enrich their mind
To grow and mature
As a good fruit would do
Love and affection
Will see them
Blossom
Their minds are so fragile
As the velvety petals of flowers
Will collapse
If fed with hate
Mistrust
Will malign the affection
To make them stiff
And even unstable
In times we reason
And teach them brotherhood
We fail to remember

And have become revengeful
We poison
Their minds
With issues
They never
Comprehend
We dispute over
My tribe
Your tribe
And we forget
Our nation
My religion
Your religion
And we estrange
Our Saviour
Zealots in the mainstream
They deflate our hope
To become as one
Poverty is blind
To tribe and the aches in the stomach
The works of God
Is seamless knowing no frontiers
The borders we find
Are man-made obstacles
As a nation young
Our focus is directed
And like the star
That shines by night
Every dream in the heart of man
Will have the chance to come alive
Tolerance must be our only watch word
Not prejudice and hate
We must open the curtains in our hearts
That true light may enter
And illuminate our lives.

Adamu Ajunam

ASKIA MOHAMMED*

I am Askia Mohammed
A messenger of the people
I lie in peace my golden reward.

I will live quietly like a flake of snow
I will rekindle thoughts that all sleeping dogs will rise
I will return to see where sunset glows like burning fire
I will come to see if cock crows still offer hope at dawn
I will come to see what happened to your ivory towers
I will search for our sages at Timbuktu now only shadow
I will not accept the shriveled face of a beautiful age left abandoned
I will look for the heads that will wear our coveted crowns
I will not accept the heads bowed in self-defeat and seek escape
I am ridiculed and must find when the chicken ate the lion's heart?
You have surrendered to poverty and suffer emptiness.

I am Askia Mohammed
A messenger of the people
I lie in peace my golden reward.

In your lands of plenty, poverty is still a public enemy
Your walls are stained with blood from wars
Great leaders have disappeared like pin in the hay
Not even the freedom many died for is anymore secure
Children have lost their tongues from wars and lost their say
Others have lost their limbs and cannot help build tomorrow
Children pointing guns against each other claiming enemy
Your brother worse than the church rat can not be your enemy
The one used unkindly as a slave can not be your enemy
Your burden is the heavy cloud that will not clear
Your enemy is the ignorance cunningly robbed

I am Askia Mohammed
A messenger of the people
I lie in peace my golden reward.

Hope has been devoured by mental delusion
The race for riches has become unstoppable
Eating deep in the psyche of even your toddlers, regrettable
If children become all corrupt, tomorrow is lost forever.
I see a ship in the horizon drifting on its way to wilderness
And I realize the time has come for my spirit to be born again
I will resurrect our dreams and invite our ancestors
To make our dreams deep rooted
And our children must awaken to enemies only imagined
The sun shall rise again across the land
You will walk bathed in the warmth of its gold into a new dawn.

*Mohammed Ben Abu Bekr or "Askia The Great", was a great King of the Songhay Empire in the 16th century. It was during his time that Timbuctu became known as a centre of learning.

Adamu Ajunam

THE GATES OF KANO CITY

The gates they opened
To welcome their friends
The gates they shut
To defend their land
The gates the king passed
To swell his kingdom
The gates no one manned
Until it turned to the gate of intolerance.

The gates that stood
Between brothers
Like China wall
Bitterness stood
Like an unconquerable mountain
The gates through which rays of hope passed
That reason may return anew
The gates that rain-washed
The walls of blood and hate away.

Now time has withered all barriers
And ushered in the age of brotherhood
The gates that opened like the wings of a dove
To embrace the humble spirit of Mallam Aminu Kano
Who reached the poor and the oppressed
Provided succour for their grief
Displaced the hate they carried within
And planted hope to grow forever
The gates have now widened
To welcome every child.

THE ATILOGWU DANCER*

Echoes of the drum pulsate the air
It is beckoning the hearts of the young and graceful
The sonorous whistling of the birds is echoed by the flute
As the metal gong rings to thaw the frigid bodies
From the rich percussion of dry cherry seeds
Echoes the sweet and jolly sound of the Atilogwu music.

It is the dance of the young and lively
Clad in petals that shine like the sunflower at dawn
With girls whose breasts flow only with innocence
And boys who overleap with joy in their hearts
All adorned with the crown of feathers of the flamingo
Echoes of the sweet and jolly sound of the Atilogwu music

From the overflow of the colourful rhythm
The nippy movement of youthful dancers
The depth of fountain of joy they spread to all
And the uniqueness of the black that cover their skin
I rejoice that hope has come alive
Echoes of the sweet and jolly sound of the Atilogwu music.

*Atilogwu dance is a dance full of acrobatic display common with the Ibo youths of the Eastern part of Nigeria.

Adamu Ajunam

MY PEARL

I have been through
The blistering cold
I have been burnt
By the scorching sun
I have walked through
The rains that washed my tears
I now know the nakedness
Of a dejected heart
I know the pain,
I know the ache
I know the anguish
Of a lonely heart
I feel deserted among a million
I feel the weight,
I feel the burden
Carried by a million heads
Resting on my tiny shoulder
The flashes of the old
Do bring some sorrow
And boil over the head.
The tear drops
 Dig a furrow
On my pitiful face
When love and harmony
Were with me
My heart was covered
Like a beautiful garden.
Forget me not,
Carnation, roses and more
Flourished in me
Life oozed
With your sweet perfume
Precious moments
When I carried you
In my hands

And suddenly my pearl disappeared
Drafted by the gale
I will not stop and stare like a captured zombie
My heart will pursue
The gale and never rest
I have left my fears
And will not be imprisoned
By this ferocious snarl
I know how to stop.
This wicked misdirected wind
I will follow
Until it loses her swirl
To find my pearl
And smile again.

Adamu Ajunam

PHANTOM COUP

When rats become esteemed
And the ridicule of their presence is welcome
When the way of goats
Become preferred to the wisdom of the ants
When ranting turns profitable
And truth must hide in shame
When the politicians go to town
And build their empty castles
When the truth become distorted
That the followers do not see their doom
Only to stray naked into the market place
When Lilliputians become taller than giants
And dwarfs enjoy the accolades of champions
When the spineless citizens
Become the backbone of a nation
And uprightness is regarded as senselessness
When moralists find soul mates in crooks
And decadence becomes the order of the day
When the blind become the light bearers
And pitfalls become normal walk
When gangsters become role models
And the real gems take the backstage
When lack of plan yields only failure
And the architects turn to heroes
When chaos becomes a lifestyle
And right is claimed by the law of the jungle
When a few suffer delusion
And the nation is caught in a web
When the visionaries become indifferent
And the tears of their pain become unnoticed
When the waiting for the dawn becomes endless
And evil seems to win at every level.

THE IDLER

Providence visited a land of plenty
Where wealth covers the land like carpet grass
And stock will graze in winter's absence
Where milk could flow not only from coconut trees
And mothers would never fear
The gruesome claws of hunger
But nourish from the grace of nature
The gods however do not allow
Providence touched each door
To bless like Santa Claus
Everyone climbed the back of fate
To pull each one a wish
Good fortune and a bed of roses
Silver spoons and golden ones were all to offer
To all who a little struggle
One lot was curiously within
Slamming the door on the face of fortune
I checked deep into their well
It was dry like desert sand.
They float like cotton seeds
And idly dream all day
They come like leeches or parasites
Their daily routine bears no difference
To strive to get by the day like dead wood
Employing self miserly or plotting chaos
Without regard for self-esteem
They emulate the habit of vultures
That feed only on carcass
To be cynical about labour
But survive from the gains

Adamu Ajunam

Falling only from manna
They employ folly
And the elegance of knavery
To survive and complete the day
And wallow without self-pity
The waste valves they are.
Providence we implore to overlook
And send us the mighty rain.

GOOD MORNING

The cock is an early riser cackling delightfully
It speaks the language of every tongue
Announcing the dawn of a new day
It is the first to see hope in the rising sun
Welcoming the spirits from the journey
Where souls are made anew
It is flapping its wings
To fan the embers
That the spirits will glow from the well of life
And drink from the promise of the rising sun
It is warning all those who delay
To make haste before the well runs dry
It is decoding with her crowing
The message of a new day
It is asking to forget the pitfalls of yesterday
And wear the heart of a child
Devoid of prejudices and burden of envy
It is rejoicing about the sorrow
That got lost in the dark of the night
The crowing of the cock is loud and clear
Dismissing idleness and inherent fears
All dark clouds do not muster to become storm
The cock is an early riser cackling delightfully
It speaks the language of every tongue
It is decoding with her crowing
The message of a new day
It is always wishing a brand new day
A universal song to every land.

Adamu Ajunam

AREA BOY

The child whose birth was much expected
The arrival that ended all anxieties
The child who was born and fit to go
The child as gentle as a little lamb
The child that grew and turned to become uncanny
The mother who saw and drowned in sorrow
The father who will not halt the sinking boat
The street that leads to no destination
In the city where the mighty care less for the feeble
The bridge in the city that became home
The child that suffers rejection
The child that makes the city a jungle
The drugs that turns him to a hooligan
The guns the child gets as gifts
The innocent who die from his gun
The child who has become as cold as stone
The city that has lost its glory
The child who lost his conscience
The child who bathes with blood
The city that will only cry wolf
The child the city turned into an urchin

THE LOCUST YEARS

You are a nation dear to the Almighty
Endowed with unlimited favour
Basking in the sun that freed you from bondage
And buoyed by waters that never run dry

The size of your nation
Evokes fear among equals
Your natural endowments
Stir envy among the rich

You boast about your land of great potentials
When will you wake and redeem your greatness?

When doors were shut and opportunities so shallow
When dreams were misty and hope was hopeless
When slave drivers captained your ship
And abandoned the hull in the open ocean

You gained your freedom without the war cries
Unlike your brothers who swallowed cannon balls
Your ship was rescued from deep waters
Captained by men who saw the future in the morning sun

You boast about your land of great potentials
When will you wake and redeem your greatness?

The milk from the breast of our motherland
Our forbearers drank to escape uncertainties
The new generation drinks the same
But journey deeper into the jungle

Your children have grown to become like locusts
They have not become foxes to lead through the night
They have come of age not carrying the lion's heart
And our ship is threatened to return to the wilderness

Adamu Ajunam

You boast about your land of great potentials
When will you wake and redeem your greatness?

I am afraid one rotten apple corrupts the basket
An alarming cancer for a nation in the storm
Deceit has snapped the binding thread
And trust has sunken deep the calamity

Some children are blinded by insincerity
Becoming only apprentices in the devil's workshop
Others have crossed the threshold and only conspire
In friendship that is the great gift of all

You boast about your land of great potentials
When will you wake and redeem your greatness?

www.ingramcontent.com/pod-product-compliance
Lightning Source LLC
Chambersburg PA
CBHW031258290426
44109CB00012B/633